Confessions to Cierra

Confessions to Cierra

by

Imy Verjee

1stBooks – rev. 9/19/00

To the Reader

This collection of writings I present to you, these confessions previously held hostage to privacy and solitude, as a record of my encounter with some vision I now no longer know was there. No more than one can claim that the lightning flashed much more brightly than it had before, or that the thunder rolled more deeply, at just the moment in which you turned to Heaven and asked of it one sign. Even in that moment lies the seed of doubt, and as time moves on, as days pass by, the seed begins to grow. Today, so many days gone by, the planted doubt is in full bloom. Perhaps I hadn't paid the storm much heed until that moment; perhaps I've asked for a thousand signs and hold to just one memory; perhaps she walked through one of my dreams, one which lasted night after night, and whose shadow even still claims some part of my waking mind.

I here present a tale I can no longer claim is true, only that I think I know it came to me, that vision. Only that I thought, that is I think I thought, that one day she fell into my life. And I feel this with such conviction that perhaps there never did arrive these recollected moments, for such a sense of clarity in thought has yet to reoccur, yet to reappear within a conscious state. Of late, the desire to put this record together has set itself against my nature, promising my pen some hitherto unknown opportunity for self-conquest; you will, I trust, forgive me for that degree of self-indulgence which has necessarily accompanied it. If any moral to this tale is found, I'll leave its message in your hands.

Confessions to Cierra

Imy Verjee

To Jack

I don't know man, I never did know but this: that all I've ever wanted to do was disappear. I walked around again today, all day, tonight, all night, and of course it had to rain. But still, still through all the rain you know I thought for just one moment that I saw the sun all red and burnin' and in some place I knew that sun was there and even for the rain it stayed today and stayed tonight and for the darkness of this night I think I saw the sun still red still burnin' on and on. I think it's had those days, those years, those lifetimes, too. I think the sun has had to think sometimes that all it had to do was move away was disappear. I'm quite convinced it has, it has to have, it has, it's felt that way too. But still it burns, just can't escape, for all the hours of the night somewhere there's hours of the day and never once has it just gone just run away. I don't know brother I don't know how it's managed to stay.

You're the best, man, you are not were the very best. I don't know how you did it how you trailed after all those shooting stars and still exploded with the brightest centrelight of all. I don't know how you saw what vision came to you with whose eyes you saw nor whose hand you wrote but always I am in your debt. I only hope you passed on becoming Buddha and came instead to help those still tied down and trapped on this the wrong side of the river, I only hope you've yet to leave. Sometimes, sometimes when I no longer know myself, when I don't know who I am - sometimes when I'm far from home just beaten by the road and haunted by the sky sometimes when I find four walls make up a cheap hotel room that I've never seen you're all there is beneath that strange red sun you're all that keeps familiar on that day which always comes again, on that strange red afternoon.

Confessions to Cierra

Imy Verjee

To Stacey

'Ere this kindly girl took pity on me. Very many people have thoroughly misconstrued my mind, very many people have looked at one another with shaking heads; but you, you're the only one I know who knows, who knows me. I don't keep many things, always feared that pictures froze the soul and haven't many things besides to keep. Even the mind, I find this mind betrays such memories as others hold so easily, but the first time we talked, really talked, that I do remember, that I've always kept. It wasn't the first time we met, but still it was; I remember sitting on your couch, we were sitting on your couch and I told you more than I have ever told, 'till now, 'till this. And even now and even still I did reveal to you much more on that first couch than I have any other, more than I have ever shared with one whose eyes when raised met mine.

I haven't yet discovered how it is you find such dreams, nor how it is (and this I feel I know) you'd be the lone escaping lobster from the tank, the only one with claws unbound the only one to find the door and disappear, the only one to disappear into such dreams. And caught, if caught, so you'd only be by some strange principled denial of that same door and those same dreams. Although I've never found through sleep some land replete with sunlit grass, although I've never walked beside a unicorn or some sweet angel dancing through my bedroom walls, I have born witness to a more convincing sign. For all the hours that I've laid beneath an open sky and vowed to stay until some creature born divine laid down along my side, for all the days that slowly passed me by, my trembling faith has always held its ground because of you. With words alone the world would never last, and yet when all the lives within my head refuse to close their eyes and sleep it's you I keep awake with words until such time arrives as all seems clear, until with wanting breath I fail to think of further words to say.

Confessions to Cierra

Imy Verjee

To my Confessor

By what name ought I call you? Of whom ought this tale be told? Of you, of course, but of what name? Laura? Stella? Juliet? Oftentimes I've thought perhaps that all the Fates were wrong to spin your life and mine with every stitch the same; I've thought it likely that those three were tired angels when they weaved our living thread. I've thought that just perhaps those three little words were never meant to touch your lips, to find my ears, to make complete my lost and absent soul. And then, I know it's built irrational, and then I think I hope and so I think that maybe there can be a second part to this, a second chapter of a tale that seeming bears no crack to break the dam - for faith commands no force divine be long-resisted by mere mortal dams. Therefore I still, in times of folding sanity, think that there may be some yet unseen path which leads if only dreaming to a shelter from this constant rain.

If any second chance can come to pass, and now I know so many have if made so slim. You are the only light I've known that can redeem, the only shining star when clouds of fog deny deprive disown a starless sky. No friends of slight acquaintance do I keep, for friendship is the stuff of love by Heaven sent I'm sure, yet never only friends were we no more than only bound eternal was our thread. And now no words more hollow ever have been writ, for every sun that rises red to light your sky so sets, that same sun sets to darken mine. So softly said were those three words that they were carried was itself remarkable; but even more, and more my fashioned sign, is that they echo through my mind and leave the imprint of once-blessed love to stay. What, love, what love is shared, what company is love.

Confessions to Cierra

Imy Verjee

The first-born angel softly plays her song,
Replaces night with fingers coloured red,
Floods life into the Valley of the Dead,
She breathes for me, and for her breath I long.
Green eyes that hold my mind to Love belong,
So deep and pure as seas that Venus fled;
No god in death, red blood Achilleus shed,
I mortal yield, Love's dart is true and strong.
False light dissolves, and music fades away,
Rebirth begins with hair just brushed by Dawn;
It flows like winds of time, like tears roll on
Down uncreased faces bright and fond of play.
"Awaken child, and hear Love's minstrel sing,
To win her hand you must his armour bring."

Confessions to Cierra

Sweet jasmine's scent is playful on her neck,
It draws me near, like Heaven's whitest light;
Love's slave I am, and kneel to see his knight,
For her I'd take on Cain's eternal trek.
Love's soldier comes in red, and golden flecked,
To keep the day from stealing our first night;
With his strong hand I'll win this noble fight,
Return to Eden from my earthly wreck.
Red lips, like goddess Dawn's first holy sign,
Who strokes the sky, and burns her flaming brand
Upon the seas and wind and sacred land,
Sweet Cierra's sigh makes even darkness shine.
I long for Love to be my guide and friend,
With grace from God this night will never end.

Imy Verjee

A life once born and raised is freely sent
To disappear amongst the fallen seed;
No past have I which is for her hand meant,
Each soldier once deceived will surely bleed.
My weary thoughts, replete with needless things,
Slip from my mind, by Cierra formed anew;
They fall away as she the sunlight brings,
Unspoken words are far between and few.
As for a better coat the snake will shed,
And leave its skin to feed the hungry land,
So do I rise from this cold earthly bed,
To feel the warmth of Heaven in her hand.
The step does scare, for every truth to tell,
The sun too close in flight Icarus fell.

Confessions to Cierra

With scarce a touch the gods have laid their plan,
She is the shining star at last revealed;
No longer captive is the favoured man,
Who carries Love in banner and in shield.
Each mortal sky is dulled by Heaven's light,
Now Cierra does each earthly thing eclipse;
As will true fire frozen ice ignite,
So was I made to burn for Cierra's lips.
The Seven Sleepers would awake for her,
Would leave safe mountains, chance each emperor.
We are as one, and from the world remove
The breath from air, and water from the snow;
Each swan that mates will true devotion prove,
From Heaven whispered sighs cause love to grow.

Imy Verjee

Love makes his bed within my captive mind,
He sets his soldiers out to clear the field;
No danger now of any doubt to find,
He is the only god to whom I yield.
No horse is built to my walled-town deceive,
With open gates his armies I invite;
For Cierra I with gratitude receive
The hand of Heaven, and its gift of sight.
Red Love provides the fire and the fuse,
He sets my heart aflame in sacrifice;
Complete control he takes, and plans to use,
But Cierra's heart is fair at any price.
A shepherd's tale is whispered to the sheep,
Of promises He makes but does not keep.

Full faith allows the shadows to recede,
And nevermore will they our love impede.
I have not Heaven seen until this day,
Within her reach I firm resolve to stay.
She is the rising sun to end the night,
Which held me fast for years without a light.
But now the breaking Dawn is beauty pure,
Her touch alone would every mortal cure.
I cannot think but that the gods do cry,
For she belongs amongst the Heavens high.
Yet from the Graces did she sure descend,
And fortune spins her smile to my heart lend.
In Cierra did the gods complete their task,
For men who pray, immortal visions ask.

Imy Verjee

Alone are we, within this pressing crowd,
It moves along a very different web;
Love has upon his children cast a shroud,
Which plays the tide, but fast restrains the ebb.
Each fate swift spins to hold secure this night,
Hers is the breath of Venus, Heaven sent;
No starlit sky did ever shine so bright
As her eyes do, Love has his dart well-spent.
Sweet Cierra's laugh each holy dream displays,
It soft evokes the Spirit of the Dance;
So clear that eyes do fail to find the way,
And only Love within can convince Chance.
If gracious God can hear this whispered plea,
He will descend, allow true love to be.

Confessions to Cierra

The night retains her strength, and clears the sky,
Each cloud directly learns to disappear;
Anointed now are we to feel no fear,
For Cierra even gods Olympic try.
Upon a lonely bench does Reason lie,
His strategy designed to dry the tear;
Opposing soldiers red do shine so clear
That Love consoles by moving them to cry.
Some dreams are Heaven-sent to bless the sleep,
Replenish Reason when he must retire,
They ease the troubled mind with God's caress.
Some come as Cierra has, to waking keep
In company of Love, a living fire,
With these the fortunate immortals bless.

Imy Verjee

From northern lights a summer's breeze will blow
When river Styx is touched by rain and swells;
A message sent by Love for time to slow,
At home in moonlit darkness silence dwells.
No other gift to grant but endless life,
Upon the sandy shores an angel cries;
I long for her right now to be my wife,
But every soldier falls who ill-trained tries.
The words do trip, so close and yet they fail,
On foreign soil retreat and Love betray;
I have no bread nor stones to mark this trail,
Yet from her shadow will I never stray.
The stars have moved, and hurtful Love has lied,
For goddess Dawn immortal night has died.

Dear Jack,

I am sitting here in the back of a van that picked me up about an hour ago on the outskirts of town - two Kiwis hell-bent for who knows where and an Aussie they picked up for gas money and my God I have to tell you about the most amazing blinding holy night I've ever had. I fell in love last night. Love, man, love - love that makes you want to run and jump and lie down and die and kiss the clouds and let the whole world know its true its there and everybody knows that they can be that bright blue centre-light and all they have to do is see it and you want to grab them and shake so hard they see. I swear one look - one beautiful naked spiritual look and I fell so hard I passed through every circle Dante ever dreamed. I'm writing from a van but I'm also writing from right down in the heart of the inferno - I left, you see. I mean, I walked around the town last night and talked to God and begged and pleaded and then when the sun came out I threw out my thumb again like last week and last month and last year and here I am and we'll be in another country tomorrow and she - no, She - She's there and I'm gone and I have to have some tea or something 'cause I'm twirling 'round as fast as I can and if I don't stop I swear with every lovely breath of air I'm going to fall and fall like Adam or maybe more Hephaistos but you know I'd fall from grace or lose my legs if I could just touch that face or kiss those lips or look into those glorious eyes one more time. That complete and total stranger who's changed my life and who I can say without a doubt I love and need and want to know completely.

I'm drinking now, I have to drink we haven't any tea, but what to do what can I do - She's in my head I'm on my knees I can't even think but man to hear Her voice again. She wrote Her number on my hand She (her name's Cierra) made me crazy in love and then wrote Her number and you know I want to get it tattooed right there just like it is and I want to get out right now and walk back to town and call Her up and pledge eternal love and settle down right there forever and never leave just stay and dig this life the way we always said we did but now I know I never knew.

My hands they're shaking and we, we're blowing, down some highway and the sun's just peaking and I swear I'm bursting. You know I can't imagine how it's been nineteen years (twenty soon) and I've never known love like this was real and true never wanted to live so much and die so much and scream and fly and man if I could be in your room right now if we could talk, the things to say like all the shooting stars that burn and burn to see the other side. If only I could bring Her to you - you'd see how I fell so far in love and you'd have to know that God is real and digs your life and man if I could I'd freeze this frame and stay.

I'm quite dizzy now from writing and drinking and flying down the road and turning 'round and 'round to find a way - She's in my head and heart and soul and man She's not just changed my life She IS my life She is but me I have to go because my mind is shot. I need to think and maybe watch the sky, I need to try you see just try to find that place of clarity.

Confessions to Cierra

A thief is time, to take away my light,
Now Love does rise, resplendent in his arms;
She has each won with her immortal charms,
The spinning Fates are left to judge the fight.
Time is the rock, denies both day and night,
Deceitful moves, it cares not that it harms;
Scylla is the rock, she mortal dreams disarms,
Swift strikes the hand that blindly greets her sight.
Love is emotion pure, without arrest,
He is well-shielded, true Amazing Grace;
Charybdis pure consumes without solace,
He burns with raw desire in his breast.
A dart well-thrown by Love may strike down time,
But oft does Justice kneel before the crime.

Imy Verjee

What more is there within for me to send,
To lovely Cierra, living beauty's name?
No fortune do I seek, nor worldly fame,
But that she would to me her favour lend.
On her eyes does immortal sight depend,
Within her beating heart eternal flame;
Her lips are coral spun, bring Venus shame,
And for her gentle touch the oak would bend.
Aurora comes in red to light the sky,
She brings new life where only ashes lie.
What more is there than Heaven can provide,
All roses made to bloom can ill compare;
God's freedom lies within her flowing hair,
No goddess lives to make a mortal bride.

Confessions to Cierra

Olympic light makes every shadow clear;
As one beneath the axe might view the crowd
And take a final look to stay cold fear,
I close my eyes, return to Love's red shroud.
Now Cierra, pure and true, does call on me,
From her wet sunlit isle she holds my heart;
I wish I had refused to turn and flee,
And pray that Love in grace forgives his dart.
Soft moonlit rivers do my dreams embrace,
With holy songs the Muses Cierra bless;
Amongst Elysian Fields she'll take her place,
For Venus does her countenance caress.
No eagle sent by Jove a message bears,
To prove as her eyes do that Heaven cares.

Imy Verjee

Sweet relics live so long as God allows,
O'er distant waters may He mist disperse;
Although mere mortal men are bound by vows,
With but a wave He can dispel the curse.
To Love I've burned in earthly sacrifice,
All that my kingdom holds to touch her hand;
Not even life immortal could entice
Ulysses from the call of wife and land.
So do my dreams of Cierra beckon me,
To stay this voyage and return to Love;
Her grace is in God's very company,
In beauty she eclipses every dove.
No plea of Venus made with true intent,
Can fail to gain her mercy and consent.

Confessions to Cierra

His eyes have seen the ancient world aflame,
Red Love no longer can afford to kneel;
With each caress of memory I feel,
Another tear will fall to feed his shame.
The gods immortal bow before her name,
Slow birds, like leaves that passing time reveal,
Soft sing for Love to answer my appeal,
In needful times the child of Heaven came.
So must he come in arms to win her heart,
For Cierra is beyond my mortal reach;
But Love is born to burn while others preach,
In Cierra's name he bids each ocean part.
The Dawn now Dusk, Love takes his worthy stand,
And to his slave he brave extends the hand.

Imy Verjee

I cannot think but that the Fates do cry,
That trembling Love would freeze my flaming heart;
As God for Moses bade the oceans part,
The ancient Sun sure burns salt water dry.
Apollo and his arrows never lie,
So has the archer Love fashioned this dart;
On earthly canvass she is divine art,
No mortal man can Heaven's call deny.
Unbounded hair that flows with Dawn's caress,
To shoulders bright with Aphrodite's touch,
For Cierra even broken hearts still ache.
As Venus did her son Aeneas bless,
So has her song provided me this much,
A goddess oft some maiden's guise will take.

Confessions to Cierra

The cabin bare, and I do take my leave,
Good friends I've made, but Love I'll not deceive.
With sack replete, once proffered is goodbye,
No tears are shed, for spirits never die.
A backward glance now turns and is full view,
Retraced are steps, well-lit on Heaven's cue.
Abandoned roads are paved with holy stone,
To spinning Fates I pray, the dice are thrown.
Hyperion shines on in majesty,
I am for Cierra as she is for me.
In lands most high, their beauty yet so pale,
Each poet yields before a Muse's tale.
Love at the helm, I need no other guide,
For at his will all gates swift spring aside.

Imy Verjee

To faithful memory I make this vow,
That Cierra will complete my life once more;
No other god can hold possession now,
For Love has brought this castaway to shore.
In dreams she draws me close with whispered song,
The Graces from her beauty bend away;
To her immortal heart I do belong,
For goddess Night is lost without the day.
With every lonely breeze I feel her touch,
Fast beating is my heart which cries her name,
I kneel in prayer, ask of Love this much,
That he will make the jealous suitors tame.
As did Ulysses brave the raging sea,
Such sacrifice I pledge for love to be.

Confessions to Cierra

The poet did from nature shy retreat,
When he would summer and its day compare;
She was more lovely than its changing beat,
In light eternal did his mistress share.
Hyperion slow burned his love to fall,
Now yellowed are the leaves which mark his grave;
But he the angels knew, and heard their call,
It plays immortal, echoes in the cave.
No pen as his have I for words to flow,
But Love has made his bed within my breast;
With every Muse's tale true love to show,
My hands in Heaven with the poet rest.
So long as men can breath, or eyes can see,
So long lives this, my life I give to thee.

Dear Stacey,

You won't believe me sister, and you'll never guess where I am. Okay, all right, you'll probably guess. You probably will, you see, because I've found that place we always talked about. That place Jack always tried to teach about, and lived in through benzedrine visions of Heaven and meditation ecstasy. You will recall that at the last note I was about to venture into the town of Edinburgh, delivered there by two young prophets of the South Pacific. Well, it wasn't very many days gone by before I realised that there was nothing I could do. There was no way, that is, that I can live, but am instead bound and tied and sentenced without appeal. Bound by stale air, unless; tied by stale bread, unless; and sentenced to stale thought, unless. The only way, it is the only way, unless. I had to come back, and just this very day, and just this very hour, and very nearly to this very minute did I step off the bus and here I am. And if only she would come down the street as she came down from Heaven, and if only she would take my hand again. If only we could be complete and be, and be. I picked up the phone just now, and set it down again. I have her number here, and the phone beside me, but sister, every time I look at it, it starts shaking. And God, she's so sweet I find I'm shaking too. I have to know her, I do, I know that. I have to feel her in the air, and know she feels for me - it's just like the falling rain, so clean and pure. But now I'm so close to everything, and with the thought of hearing her voice one more time, it's so close to being It, and living is so close to being Life.

I saw the sky today, I mean I laid down on the grass and stared; I just stared to see the sky, and my God did you ever know there was a sky like that? The sun and clouds, and the little white trail left behind an airplane just goin' and goin' and blowin' and blowin' across the sky. I swear I saw the world inside that sky, and lying on the ground like that, just staring at the sky, I thought about how close it really is. And I lifted my hands, my darlin' I swear I touched the clouds and felt the sun. I swear I kissed the air, and felt just a little piece of Heaven. Right then I knew, I did, I knew the world keeps spinning around, and never does stop, but for just the very minute that you raise your hands, and the very minute that you live and breath, you can be. You can be love, and have love; you can be the sky, and have the sky. And you can know, and be, and live - and live like every life is meant to live, forever. You can be with God, and you can be God, and man I have to go, because you see I have to be, and so I have to call, and so we have to see. We do, we do, we have to see.

Imy Verjee

She is the light which feeds this starving earth,
First sight again, her eyes do capture mine;
No child of nature born can meet her worth,
In Cierra's smile I see the Heaven's shine.
She is the rain which falls on desert sand,
First sight again, her lips by Venus blessed;
As God did lend Perpetua His hand,
So does she now forgive my sins confessed.
Hers is the love that bears Heavenly bliss,
First sight again, her spirit blinds the sun;
Eternal courtship for a single kiss,
Would be fair pledged, a noble fate well-spun.
In beauty she is such that none compare,
The Siren while in song is not so rare.

Confessions to Cierra

In armour clad, and with a satin shield,
Love builds his fortress in my softened breast;
Now plundered is my once well-guarded chest,
Each sacred Muse-inspired dream revealed.
To ceaseless Love I can but pray and yield,
His soldiers confident support my quest;
Without a thought to leisure or to rest,
Red armies build a stronghold in this field.
Anointed lovers brave become the shark,
And ever-forward move with God as guide,
Cold faceless Death will come if they are still.
To light they flow, slow struggle in the dark,
But Cierra of the Graces does not hide,
Her brilliance takes firm hold and is Love's will.

Imy Verjee

Upon her hair she wears Aurora's crown,
And with a golden head the arrow flies;
Eternal Heaven burns this mortal town,
Soft Cupid rises, strength in love supplies.
When proud Adonis bent to draw his bow,
It was from Venus that he turned away;
But never made was buck, nor ever doe,
For which he would from Cierra's presence stray.
So brilliant is her light, each ember feeds,
That every Fate is spun and cut like twine;
Lord Helios, with chariot and steeds,
Is made a shadow, she was born to shine.
No lead is built into his truest dart,
Red Love has struck, and Cierra is my heart.

Confessions to Cierra

Green eyes that shine so bright they dull the day,
Make every sun eclipse and moon withdraw;
She looks at me, and Love invokes his law,
He keeps his slave in blindness, lights the way.
No chance to speak, for Love swift from me strays,
Removed from him I shake like wind-blown straw;
Afraid to meet her gaze, love's greatest flaw
Is cowardice, which on sweet lovers preys.
And yet beloved Cierra is so near,
That I must take this stand and voice my thoughts;
In Love's most sacred web I have been caught,
In day or night her face alone is clear.
Eternal life amongst the gods is fine,
But death on earth I'd choose if she were mine.

Imy Verjee

No silence ever came so soundlessly,
As Love's true dart does on my target land;
In pouring rain pure fire takes its stand,
Once broken wings can fly at God's decree.
Her shining eyes, like spirits of the Cree,
Can see flames doused with ashes, dust, and sand;
Forgive me life, I'd leave you for her hand,
Her fingertips dance out my destiny.
Love's drug of choice is ecstasy so true
That every hit removes God's gift of life,
It cuts through hearts like Brutus' silver knife,
Yet gives the gift of Heaven as a view.
She, Cierra, is pure ecstasy with just,
The price of everlasting love and trust.

Confessions to Cierra

Cold Fear comes forth from shadows to my heart,
His arms are seas to keep our love apart.
For in one day, one week, one month alone,
Some lonesome dove will fly to call me home.
The time is short, yet how can I reveal,
To my true love the anguish that I feel?
For fortune's sake I'll hold my tongue and kiss
The Dawn in Love's most sacred warmth and bliss.
Her hand on mine feels like an angel's wing,
Stirs every creature's heart, makes Heaven sing.
Full moon above, yet wolves refuse to cry,
In dread of catching Cierra's burning eye.
But softly creeping is Fear's soldier now,
He strives to betray Love and break my vow.

Imy Verjee

Uncertainty aside, Love regains hold,
And passing time is held still in its track;
Like sunlight dancing now upon my back,
She is the flame which heats this life so cold.
An oak will break, but never ever fold,
Nor will Love's armour fail and show a crack;
Prometheus upon the torture rack
Would stay man's fire for her hands to hold.
So must I now refuse to bend and ply,
But rather stand in Love's protective ranks;
So confident are preachers who give thanks,
Yet with one dart Love can evoke their cry.
A captured hen will give the fox her life,
So do I pledge to Love this sacrifice.

Confessions to Cierra

Some lovers speak, they turn to poetry,
Of hopes and fears and unknown desire;
Of hellish pain, and pleasure heavenly,
Of living deaths, fair storms and freezing fire.
Some think of Jove, and all his strange attire,
Dressed up as bulls and swans and golden rain;
More modest men to open fields retire,
And bring Love's royal thoughts upon the plain.
To some the Muses sing and grace afford,
Tears born of ink show sighs at every word.
Wet paper pale despair, with pain will move,
I speak I feel, and feel as much as they;
But think that all the words I can display,
With trembling voice that I do Cierra love.

Aligned are they, the sacred stars of life,
Each takes the side of Love the feuding soul;
Atop his throne as bearer of the knife,
Is golden Jove, immortal yet not whole.
First Venus with her swans upon the stage,
The mark of Cierra branded on her shield;
Yet Fear does taunt the senses in my cage,
And Darkness of Unknowing is revealed.
The second seat belongs to Demeter,
She begs me pause for love of blood and land;
Still Risk arrives, and Cowardice with her,
No armies do await a shy command.
The father Jove is blind but cannot see,
His justice is restrained and will not be.

Confessions to Cierra

Dear Jack,

How can I write how can I write my God sweet pure and gracious God how can I write a note to even Jack, my blood my bro my finest written word how can this be? What spell was cast what curse was laid what did I do, and in this endless night that fell and fell like every sky came crashing down to fall somehow I have this pen to hold and if it wasn't here I don't know where I'd be, but please forgive me man I have a tale to tell and God in Heaven please allow I tell it brave and tell no lie because, because the tree can't blame the leaves for fallin', and I have none to blame for blowin', but I did oh yes indeed I did. I blew, I did, and left the dust to fight and kick up high and man I'm back in this dear land we all call home but she - but She - she's gone all gone. Oh man, to keep and be specific, in the interest of the art, she stayed and me, I failed, it's me that's gone. I'm mad, I've gone quite mad, of this I'm sure because the little piece of us that keeps us sane and keeps us right and keeps us on that yellow road it's in that little town and in that little girl who gave me God and in her hands I placed my heart and mind and with the last the mind so went my little spark of sanity.

I woke on the day, that last most glorious day, and see I had my ticket home and so I had to go I couldn't stay but man those summer nights just fell away and all the truth and those two eyes they closed and so did I. I couldn't stay but if I could and hell of course I could I could 'cause brother mine she's all there is and very nearly did I approach and ask for bus fare back in trade for going home (the dear sweet lady at the airline counter just smiled like she knew and smiled that warm smile and though she knew she smiled and never have I seen such sadness in a smile) . Very nearly, so they say, but nearly ain't, just plain ain't, and so I step on homeland soil and so I close this first and last and every chapter. Now all the concrete glass of the city is groanin' and every willow tree is cryin' and even the air itself is chokin' and me I'm here and God if I could be. At least a bird can say to hell with flight and drop into the canyon or the sea at least a turtle has a shell an ostrich has the sand but me I'm lost or trapped or trapped somewhere I'm lost and why but who can say but me and all I say to mean and all I think to say is why?

You've got to know, you know, know when to hold on, that's all I know now, too little and too late to do more than say, but though its meaning has been stripped it's all that's true. You got to know when to hold on so tight the blood leaves your hands and you feel each heartbeat - and man I laid down on the morning grass today and thought and dreamed and left to be with her again, I held so tight I heard her catch her breath at the lightning flash and felt her hip beneath my hand just resting felt like we'd been cast and shaped and tempered but now the one has split and now the one is far divided (exactly nine hours and nine minutes of miles, including the necessary delays of bus and customs check) and I have just this pen and every drop of dew beneath my head was just another tear from Mother Earth and Cierra has to know I never meant for this but man oh man what fitting empty words to end an empty and far worse a broken-down defence.

Confessions to Cierra

The pyramids were made of stone to last,
On hallowed ground they stand as seasons turn;
With such a wall to keep mere mortals fast,
Each buried god is safe, their fires burn.
Like some new Cleopatra come to rule,
Whose beauty did win both great emperors,
Has Cierra set aflame the flowing fuel
Which feeds each heart, God's own keeps time with hers.
In vibrant life the Heavens Cierra shield,
Their wall is cast from high on Muse's hill;
Divinity on earth in her revealed,
With but a glance all thunderclouds are still.
White feathers fall from doves up in the sky,
They dance around the clouds to catch her eye.

Imy Verjee

To Cierra form are holy flowers three,
Which cure the earth, relieve the sullen bell;
Within her body does the shamrock dwell,
And so provides in her the Trinity.
Now sinless mind, the Tao has made it free,
Her will alone would undo Circe's spell;
Upon her birth the jewelled lotus fell,
To bless her thoughts with divine purity.
The flowing life of Cierra is complete
With love beyond Erato and her song;
A myrtle laid within does blossom strong,
Three Graces for its favour fierce compete.
Perfection is this loving flower child,
Her charm would freely tame Charybdis wild.

Confessions to Cierra

The goddess Dawn brings forth another day,
Her dancing light shines on a sleeping sea;
Like nature's gifts of sun and moon and tree,
She is God's first and perfect use of clay.
As darkness fades, bright angels guide her way,
Before her step cold shadows turn and flee;
Burnt offerings by suitors made in plea,
Creation sings, and for her glance all pray.
Though oftentimes I've held her in my mind,
As children do, with candles for the year,
They hold the wish for God above to hear,
I cannot in this darkness daylight find.
Though Aphrodite's path is laid with love,
Hephaistos' chains have bound her from above.

Imy Verjee

Feel and oh sensation,
River flowing from Creation.
Spin wild for spinning light,
Cut gloves, the loser of the fight.
Too many arrows fly,
But nerve to hold is not to cry.
A sun that sets is done,
Embrace so others hateful shun.
Come God and let me kneel,
Allow the pain within to feel.
I was not born to die,
But rather meant to kiss the sky.
Just one last word so weak,
The axe is cut to slay the meek.

Confessions to Cierra

Now hidden is the Muse,
Just singing blues.
A closing open door,
Upon the poor.
Within the pouring rain,
The turning brain.
No fence is so well-built,
Of sand or silt.
The light of Heaven cast,
Was not to last.
True love the vicious lie,
Does life deny.
Immortal Cierra came,
A crying shame.

When with a lonely cry the wolf retreats,
And from the farmer flees possessed by fear,
It is the blood of life turned empty streets,
Perhaps it is the thunder cracking clear.
As every wolf endangered have I fell,
From Heaven's light to this cold barren place;
Within the valley deep I hapless dwell,
To cling forever to her holy face.
But in the shadows lies another trap,
By every angry Fate the chains are laid,
Intent they are to break the broken mind.
With Cierra did I lie in Heaven's lap,
And every debt to God is yet unpaid,
To pay the price Cain roamed to never find.

Confessions to Cierra

The prophet sits upon a mountain high,
And gazes down on land he has let see;
His only thoughts to set his children free,
No broken Fate can make conviction shy.
No savage wind displaces planted seed,
Torrential rain cannot his fire wet;
Though every trial of Job is Heaven set,
He sees that love fulfils our every need.
Yet now the sun slow fades into the night,
Its sacrifices spent are paid no heed,
When gods and devils fight for sinful pride.
With love is brought the living death of sight,
And golden darts let fly cause lovers bleed,
The prophet from his altar candid lied.

Imy Verjee

A single tear by Heaven shed soft rolls,
From cloudless skies a thousand drops of rain;
They douse no flames and do not soothe the pain,
Off in the distance close a bell slow tolls.
Each diamond bright has been reduced to coal,
Lie left abandoned, do invite disdain;
All prayers empty, offered each in vain,
Once broken circles never become whole.
The Fates have cut my thread and cast it clear
Of Cierra's life, my one desired end,
Without her love mine is a cursed trek.
Not even Hermes golden-clad is near,
My soul is lost, no god will guidance send,
Nor protest at the noose around my neck.

Confessions to Cierra

Come forward Cierra, please I need you now,
In this cold empty night I know not how.
No peace to make with sleep, she will not fall,
And with the break of day I hear no call.
In silence every bird has left the sky,
My life is hardened every time I try.
Without a sun to shine or air to draw,
Love is no longer, nor immortal law.
Forsaken on my knees I beg her hear,
True love is ill-protected from this fear.
Each passing night her hand does slip from mine,
Now even dreams do capture and confine.
Another staring contest with the flame,
It burns on still, but fire bears no name.

Imy Verjee

Dear Stacey,

Dear Stacey, oh dear oh dear - I must confess to you a sin, one most vital to this note and better said at this most early stage. Yes, I do have a confession, sister, and I think perhaps I may have more than one. Seven days and seven nights it has most surely been. One week, and full and most complete of sleepless visionary existence, with one meal a day to temper hunger pangs and only drink to drink. Only drink, because they say *in vino veritas,* and I have found that only drink can fuel the sober mind. The meal is slight and made to cleanse, because I've found that with a brief reminder every hunger stays as hunger, and will stay instead of fading into a dreamlike numb submission and acceptance of the fast. I have not smoked tobacco in this week, and find the conflict almost just too much to bear, and yet it feeds upon and also provides food. It brings the stuff of pain and longing in the body, one which imitates - if only poorly - the pain and longing of my essential mind.

This confession made I must reveal the deeper nature of this note. Kid, I'm so scared right now I have to drink, if only so that when I die, I can die, and die in truest form, with an open mind if slow to meet the non-existent death. In such a tempered temperamental state as this I have to try to make myself precise. I love. I do, I love, but love me, there is the harm. You see them, I know, I know you do and I see them too, the blind young children of this world, the loveless people who non-exist to drain the very life essence of a passive soul, they clog the roads less travelled by with broken carts and rubbish strewn - and as for that far more chosen path, it simply leads into their fortified communities. There, you are doomed or better damned to lose your mind, and gain in forfeit only their sheep-like responses and sheep-like state of mind.

But me, not me, I love, I know I do because of that gone little girl of whom I have written throughout the summer months in which love naturally comes to bloom. You know what, forget it, it's already gone and so am I.

Confessions to Cierra

A moonlit night will house forgotten dreams,
For those who missed the cut of Cupid's dart;
Unbroken skin defends a broken heart,
And into life lord Ares' soldier screams.
His only thoughts are of cascading streams,
Of honey, milk, and fruit both sweet and tart;
Not of accursed lovers kept apart
On painted vases casting unlit gleams.
But those struck down by Love have more to lose,
Dressed up in red, and naked to the Fates,
No angel sings, no fire burns inside.
Cold empty thoughts from every conquered Muse,
From Heaven drift, and settle missing mates,
For cheating Love does from his lovers hide.

Imy Verjee

Aurora dressed in red, reveals another day,
To burn her flaming brand upon another sleepless night.
The waking birds that sing, are life reborn in day,
And each will thankful soar into the sky obscured by
night.
As every serpent hides, that fears the break of day,
So do I crawl within cold sheets and wait for falling
night.
The sun does not exist, there is no warmth of day,
Sweet Cierra only comes in dreams descending in the
night.
The faceless crowds will walk, slow scattered by the
day,
But each is cloaked in shadows cast by this eternal night.
In Cierra's company I did rejoice in day,
But now solace is only found beneath the shield of night.
I pledge the blood of life, to gods who bring this day,
If only I can have to hold her hand for one more night.

Confessions to Cierra

Twirling 'round and 'round inside my head
Are Muses' songs and rain with Heaven's salt;
So lonely are the crowds within this bed
That even Love the hypocrite begs halt.
And yet what other form of god to take
Would bandage such a wound so raw within?
To lift from shoulders bare all mortal ache
Accursed Atlas would repent his sin.
Outside the sun and moon for rule fierce fight,
While Love and Ares always had a pact;
Within the mortal falls, fate has the night,
No chance have I, for every deck is stacked.
Blindness for the blind is no distress,
But sight once found and lost does inward press.

Imy Verjee

A tree is lost which by the wind is cut,
So rooted now is Love from banners red;
Each window and each doorway barred and shut,
His heart betrayed, the treacherous have fled.
Unbroken darts do disappear in cloud,
Alone he is and old, God made him blind;
A fallen star in silence is so loud
That broken Love will never Heaven find.
No more distress, nor drama for the gods,
Who laugh at Love, made mortal by his pain;
See Jove himself, so cowardly he nods,
As though he fears to earn a god's disdain.
In times of peace the soldier inward dies,
So Love torments each heart when Heaven lies.

Confessions to Cierra

A mortal man will die,
His mortal god will lie.
In every sleeping child,
Is madness in the wild.
With bread turned into stone,
The preacher walks alone.
His angry tombstone calls,
Yet blindly Adam falls.
She is the only one,
I am the fallen son.
And Ocean in between,
Denies our love has been.
The passing of the time,
Is drowned by blood for wine.

Imy Verjee

A lying doctor to his patient tells,
That all is fine within the wind-torn heart;
An actor brings no justice to his part
When soft he cries, alone the church-bell knells.
Along an empty shore lie broken shells,
Struck down, each worth a single bloody dart;
The gods have but a passing thought to art,
Red Love deny each time Charybdis swells.
No demons like the ones Olympic born,
Who laugh and joke along with sweet Despair;
Come forth ye gods and breath this earthly air,
Perhaps the taste will kill your haughty scorn.
But courage never was an honoured trait,
Amongst the gods who spin a mortal's fate.

Confessions to Cierra

A shadow on the water bears no weight,
Illusions disappear into the night;
Red Love has turned, another trap to bait,
Charybdis swells, alone I unarmed fight.
This crew is one, no captain and no ship,
With only Cierra in my mind as guide;
Love had his way, my blood upon his lip,
He has with whispered sigh true love denied.
Now dolphins rise from seas to raise a cry,
And warn me of the stormclouds gathering;
Yet even as I learn love is a lie,
To faith in God and Cierra do I cling.
When faced with tasks unfit for mortal men,
Brave Heracles did meet the lion's den.

Imy Verjee

So cold it burns, the broken hand to take,
That once was set by Love himself aflame;
No longer does he wish this heart to claim,
But moves away, another dart to make.
No gods Olympic act for mortals' sake,
And when we fall they do forsake the blame;
Love turns his head to view another game,
To those who have not ever been awake.
Yet every song is known to gods above,
It is within their hands, the Fates to turn,
Our wine is water just, and bread a stone.
On bended knee again I pray to Love,
A candle wet can still by Graces burn,
No fire built by gods is sent alone.

Confessions to Cierra

No more will he allow the chips to fall,
Who to forsaken dreams withholds the key;
Each broken mirror, lonely company,
Does blindly stare before the spinning ball.
Around it goes, born running meant to crawl,
Breeds bloodless lips that move in silent plea;
The lover left with nervous smoke to see,
I am alone within this mad chagall.
Here Cierra comes, in flowing bridal dress,
Her hand in mine brings every warmth of Dawn,
And this fast-spinning serpent I deny.
The truest love is felt in her caress,
In her green eyes the face of God is drawn,
I turn to Cierra as the mirrors die.

My dearest Cierra,

It's been two years now, since that night, that first night. It's been two years since that week, that world-stopping week. Two years. Two years of waking up and holding my eyes shut real tight, just praying that when I'd open them, when I'd open them I'd see you there, sitting at the foot of the bed. Two years of waking up, hoping, holding. Two years. Every morning waking up, praying that you'd be there again, that we'd have that cup of coffee, just sitting on the bed, that we'd smoke the day's first cigarette, just there. The sun coming in through the blinds. Kids out playing in the field, playing in the street, kids out playing with the sun shining in through the blinds. Two years of just trying to go back in time, just holding on, to what was there, to what we had, just there. Two years of nights spent staring at the wall, and just before daybreak closing my eyes and holding them tight, and just praying. Two years of talking to God, of asking Him for His hand, to go back. Two years of regret.

Now. Now I'm lying here in this rented room, it's four o'clock in the morning, and I don't even know what town I'm in. Just going. I miss you so much, so much, it's like I left myself behind. And I see you all the time, on those rare nights I sleep, I see you, I see you in my dreams, and every day, when I walk outside, I see you on the corner, in the store, I see you drive by, and I hear you catch your breath in every thunderstorm. There isn't a thing in the world I wouldn't give to have the chance to right my wrong, to go back, and stay. I hope you can forgive me. Cierra, I'm sorry. I got lost, lost along the way, but I know now, I only hope it's not too late. You know, you feel so empty, but you go on, because its expected of you, you go back, because its expected of you, and you follow the rules, just because its expected of you. And a year later, a year too late, I saw that being back was wrong, it was a sin - beyond sin, it was ripping me apart, and I don't know if you'll, I feel like, like I...

I was talkin' to a fellow who, we were in jail together, awhile back (he was gettin' transferred and I was servin' an unpaid ticket), and he was telling me about this, this place called Angola, down in Louisiana, this, this maximum security prison, like a work farm. And he told me that you walk in the front doors of that prison, and it's like your life is this 2000 piece puzzle, and you walk in the door, and all 2000 pieces get scattered, you get broken up, and you just disintegrate. And he told me you spend the rest of your life just trying to put the puzzle back together again, and I looked at him, and I realised. That they took away his body, they put him in a cage - for the rest of his life they put him in a cage - and then, and then he was shut down, and he was shut down from sensation. See, that old man, that old man had discovered, he found freedom. And he put that puzzle back together again, in his mind, and his mind for the first time in his life was free. The tragedy of it was, that even though he found every last piece, and even though he was complete in his mind, and he was free, and he had found a way, the way, to truly live, that even though he had discovered his mind essence, the tragedy of it is, that for the rest of his life he will be alone. And he has no one, no one with whom to share his discovery, and he has no one with whom to complete his discovery. He will never be able to experience, never live what he has found in the rebirth of his innocence.

The day I boarded the plane, the day I left and came back home, was the day my puzzle disintegrated. And every day I go outside, and I lie down on the grass, and I feel the sun or the rain or the snow. Every day I walk outside, and I appreciate the gift of sight, and I just watch the sky, and every day I appreciate sensation just, the sounds of life just, experiencing. But even though, even though every single day I feel the ground beneath my feet, and I see the, the everything, and every day I discover, life, and even though I'm a free man, and I can go anywhere, talk to anyone, just be. For every hour of every day, just as surely as that old lifer's body dies a little bit, so my mind just dies a little bit more. I love you. There's so much to say but it slips out in a rush, and all the words are only thoughts, with every thought I mean to say I love you.

Imy Verjee

And so, a year after the fact, having thoroughly fallen from the graces of my past life, I abandon life, and spend it recklessly, and I become a genuine Larrimer Street bum, and Cierra, I beg you, please forgive me for that. I didn't know what else to do. And I didn't know where else to go. I know this is a poor defence, and, every day, every day, whatever new vice I had discovered - whatever they buy and sell on this forgotten corner, it just pushed the despair back one more day. That's not a word I like to use, despair. It seems it's used all too often, by those who really don't deserve to use it, but I don't know another word so suited as this. Despair. And it's not sweet, whatever the poets may write, and there is no pleasure in the pain. But you know what, I look around at the people I know, and see, it's like, everywhere you look, and with everyone you know, you always see false love, false prophets with false messages, false love. You always see just a poor facsimile of love. But every morning when I go out, go face that world again, I look for love, one more time I look for love, and you look into their eyes, these lovers' eyes, and you have to shake your head and wonder why. Don't they know, don't they understand what it can be? Then again, every night I, I try to fall asleep and, and I don't even have the pretence of love, and no hope that is does, or did, or will exist. But you. But for you, you who came, and is, and you, everything you.

Sometimes you do see it you know, not often, but sometimes you do, you see lovers and you know, and you look, you look them in the eye, you look them in the eye and you can see the light, or you can, you can see that light there that, that just burns, and you know, and you know. You are that light, Cierra, only you. There are so few people in this world, that will ever find. You know, you stay up all night, and, every night, and you get to be familiar with all the television evangelists, television preachers that come at you, and they talk about experiencing the love of God, and they talk about having seen His light, and having felt His warmth, and they talk about being at one with Heaven. And you know, if I believed for a moment that they have seen in God what I see in you, that they have felt in God what I feel in you, or if I believed for one moment that their love was as genuine as mine for you, I would take great comfort in knowing, but I don't know.

The only thing that I know about Heaven is that for those five days in July I found it, two years gone by now, but I found it. I found it, and it wasn't amongst the stars, and it wasn't amongst Elysian fields, but it was with you. And every night I talk to God, and I ask Him for, I ask for love, and, and I never know if He hears me, if He's out there, if He knows; and every night I talk to you, and every night I become a part of you, and I don't know if you hear me, and I don't know if you know, but every night I try and every night it's all I can say that I am so far gone in love with you. Cierra, one more turn, and one more time the sky's just starting to brighten, and I guess, I guess I've made it through one more night. I guess we've made it through again.

Imy Verjee

When I was forced from Cierra ever dear,
Cierra, whose breath does keep my beating heart,
Cierra, whose eyes make all my shadows clear,
By iron laws of duty to depart,
I found the artist lost her love of art;
I saw that tears did in her eyes appear;
I saw that sighs her sweetest lips did part,
And her sad words my saddest sense did hear.
For me, I wept to see pearls scattered so,
I sighed her sighs, and cried before her woe,
And yet rejoiced, such love in her was seen.
Now this effect brought bitterness to me,
Though such a cause, no sweeter thing could be,
I had been tried, if tried I had not been.

Confessions to Cierra

No cloud will part when time does Love betray,
Swift golden Hermes flies with frozen wings;
Her glance alone makes peasants into kings,
Yet with my mind the doubts of distance play.
On broken sand will Love his blanket lay,
When gods above forget to push his swings;
Rose-fingertipped like Dawn, she daylight brings
For every darkened night when minds will stray.
Compare the palm tree made by God to cry,
To winged angels bathed in Heaven's light,
Or this dark corner of the Morgue of Wrath.
Alone amongst the gods I will not lie,
Nor shrink in danger's face, nor take to flight,
The spinning Fates alone adjust my path.

Imy Verjee

The hours lost in flight are hardest spent,
So slow they are to pass, like dreamless sleep,
Like prison nights with nothing to repent,
Like falling leaves, fierce fighting fall to keep.
Fair Venus and her doves upon the wing,
She has her blessing spent for love to be;
For Cierra sacred Muses nine do sing,
She has their vestal flame provided me.
Each cloud dissolving parts with thoughts of Love,
As though his dart has carved my fated way;
A single shining star burns high above,
To guide this voyage it resolves to stay.
The crashing sea upon her sacred shore,
And I have come to kneel at Cierra's door.

Confessions to Cierra

A sunlit breeze across my frozen cheek,
As that hot planet nods in warm assent;
The outskirts are reflections, it was meant
To live and breathe, Creation in one week.
For Genesis is life the lifeless seek,
And every sin I do with death repent;
To be so born as He, who Heaven sent
With words of love, to save this world so bleak.
As did Lucia bring her light divine,
So would my saint provide, her gift is mine.
I am reborn with Cierra's loving charms,
God has delivered Heaven unto me;
For love of Priam's child it was, that he
Who was immortal, died by Trojan arms.

Imy Verjee

I have no thought to sleep by day or night,
For Cierra fuels my blood with vibrant life;
Her flowing hair that dances in the light
Is Heaven cast, made free from worldly strife.
No flower blooms so lively as her lips,
Which burn to honour Dawn, who brands the sky;
Fair Venus rests her hand on Cierra's hips,
Beside the Graces does she peaceful lie.
Her eyes like gleaming stars, forever shine,
No Angel black could hope their flames to dim;
For her in circle seven would I dine,
Through burning sand would every poet swim.
A rising Phoenix is from ashes made,
New life she brings, pure sunlight through the shade.

Confessions to Cierra

I thought I saw my Cierra, maiden fair,
She wore a flowing dress, white lace to wed;
By Love she was to Heaven's altar led
And shining stars did dance about her hair.
Two Graces sat upon her shoulders bare,
The third did bind my heart, which gentle bled;
Then Cierra raised her eyes, and softly said,
Those three small words that faithful lovers share.
"I love you, I love you, I love you, dear,
To have and to hold, and always be near."
A vision Cierra is, caressed by God,
The bond of nature to Eternal Mind;
Of her sweet words there is not one to find,
With malice formed, nor with a thought to fraud.

Imy Verjee

Old tablets read, do not deceive the state,
Yet every god has Cierra made my life;
It is a trap spun carefully by fate,
That Cierra now is held fast as a wife.
She wears his ring upon her hand, and I
Am caught to fall beneath the tidal waves;
She bears his name, and in his bed does lie,
The Serpent madness loose, his guidance raves.
The truth of God now shines in naked view,
His dark deception on this day revealed;
As did the waters of Charybdis spew,
So now the demon rises, once concealed.
As one great furnace flamed; yet from those flames,
No light, but rather darkness conquest claims.

Confessions to Cierra

I saw the Roman Candle flare,
Across a starless sky so bare
It made me shake, and fall
and falling pray.

And then its bright-blue light appeared,
The startled shadows dissapeared,
And left the lives
They claimed that day.

But every shooting star is lost,
And every moment bears a cost
So dear, that even candles fade,
For flames are made to burn away.

Imy Verjee

No blacker night has ever come to be,
It drowns the jewel in a blinding sea;
Within this train, so slow it is to crawl,
Each prophet sleeps, they do relive the fall.
But for one man, who stares into the night,
And as I grieve he knows my heart by sight;
His face is hidden as he offers this,
That I should know not to surrender bliss.
And though the path may be with peril spun,
No prize claims he is without losses won;
With faith he speaks, he Heaven would invoke,
No gift from God is given to revoke.
But as this man retires into sleep,
I damn Creation, and begin to weep.

Dear Stacey,

Oh man, oh little sister, oh man. I saw the sun, see, and then wham! I went blind. I never saw another thing; got up in the morning, one morning, and like a revelation I never saw another thing. Maybe God's cuttin' back, maybe it's economics, some divine recession in the fates. Maybe the market crashed, and they're laying off, and I didn't have enough time in for this old life. Maybe I didn't have seniority. Little known fact I'll share with you, my friend, and a little known fact it is. See, the world, it's just this little tiny piece of nothin', and you and me, we're littler pieces of nothin'. And damn, whenever you get set up on your feet, and start to think that maybe there's a reason, maybe something, just then, just then, it drops the hammer down, and just laughs and laughs.

Living breeds dying, man, and the world she's spinning, but not like a top, not all crazy and out of control, it's not out of control, just out of your hands. It's like a merry-go-round, with all the horses, and all the riders. And me, I'm on the one right out on the edge, see, and that brass ring it's just there, I can see it shining and gleaming and staring and laughing, and it's there, but I can't reach it. I stand up on the horse, and I can't reach it, I pick up a stick, and I can't reach it. And you know what, that ring, that pure and divine ring, that ring that shines and says yes, absolutely yes, life and love and yes, it's just so far away, just so far that it burns itself into your mind, and then it burns the mind. Burns it up.

Everything everything everything everything - you know the old Greek gods, right, well, they have this god, and they call him Dionysus - and official titles and assignments and printed cards aside, they drown him in wine, and then they drown themselves; because the mystic spiral, it's spun out, see, and there's no lower for it to go. So you disillusion your illusions, and you live life by chasing dragons and bang! you're back, you're human all right but you're back. And maybe you're not in control, but that don't matter, because you never were, only now there's no control to be had.   Meaningless, yes, but no longer a wasteland of meaningless existence - now it's meaningless in Eden, far better than meaningless on earth. De do do do, de da da da, that's what the song says. they're meaningless and all that's true - that's all, that's everything true.

Where are you? Where are you, Stacey, are you out there? Are you really, hell, I don't know if there is an out there. Well, I hope you are, because I'm feelin' just capital, so I am. Drifting through the city streets, with a thousand city lights all flashing, and a thousand city sounds just screaming, and chaos, that's all. That's all, because that's true, at least it doesn't lie or cheat or steal. After all, there's nothing worth lying about, and nothing worth cheating for, and nothing worth stealing, because it's all mine and it's all yours. And it all belongs to chaos, it's just that no offered prayer is needed for the broken-down caves of man, or the shadows of God on the wall. It seems a contract was signed, but never delivered on, no, not so far as I can see. I did my part, oh yes I did, got born n' raised and everything, and just that taste, that little taste of Heaven. All I can say is I curse that taste, and I curse heaven. As I live and breath, my friend, no man nor god is ever going take my life again but me.

Confessions to Cierra

Immortal night descends, does day destroy,
Upon black empty fields Love walks alone;
Images of death, alive in brush and stone,
Once played upon brave Hektor's mind at Troy.
Most needful time sees Love with lovers toy,
Forgotten vows dismissed to Fates unknown;
As dying thieves will for their sins atone,
So empty words divine are but a ploy.
No god can have so hard a heart as Love,
Who sits atop his throne and fires darts;
No armour has been built to shield red hearts,
Once blind, I see the vulture in the dove.
No more ill-fated colours will I wear,
Love has no coat of arms for me to bear.

Too many times the sun would rise and fall,
Lord Helios escapes to mountains high;
Away from mortal life he hears no call
From tortured hearts that silent groan and sigh.
Red Mars is armed with soldiers passionless,
Who brave the night with armour made of bronze;
Unknown to cursed Love who'll never bless,
But rather plant the seed to burn fair lawns.
Above the sky are Deathless Ones too proud
To shed a tear for lives with which they play;
No thought spare they for those beneath the cloud,
Who cling to silver trim and kneeling pray.
Without eternal life we're spun to fail,
Love is the cross, his dart provides the nail.

Confessions to Cierra

All flames die out held fast in captive ice,
A crying child asleep and drunk on life;
Love burns its heart for one more sacrifice,
No shame has he for causing lovers' strife.
Three captured winds still blow for one more chance,
To sail this righted ship and bring me back;
False Love the crew does every wind romance,
Until cold fire fades from blue to black.
Now goddess Moon has brought an empty Night,
Would mask my path and wreck this broken ship;
No use to pray, nor offer gifts for light,
Love frolics in the blood which cut hearts drip.
Alone with Love, and Heaven's Gate is sealed,
Deceitful Fates have every stitch revealed.

Imy Verjee

Farewell, Love; and all your laws forever,
Your baited hooks shall tangle me no more,
Senec and Plato call me from your lore,
To educate my mind they endeavour.
In blind error, when I did persevere,
Your sharp rebuff, that cut me high and low,
Taught faithless vows are found in words hollow,
To escape forth, since liberty is dear.
Therefore farewell, go trouble younger hearts,
Upon me exert no more influence;
With idle youth you have predominance,
And there go spend your many brittle darts.
For now although I have lost all my time,
I care no more for rotten trees to climb.

Confessions to Cierra

Some prophet came to me in vision form,
His hands of ice he did defend as warm.
I longing looked, I did his nature see,
The black abyss, it stared back into me.
His tongue was forked, and he did hide a tail,
With lies of love he plotted me to fail.
What make of god is there who would deny
One spirit torn in two, as she and I?
Now truer words no prophet ever spoke,
As these I use to living love revoke.
His earth is built for cowardly and meek,
But through the axe the truest words will speak.
So come cold death, and test your mettle here,
I have seen God and have no other fear.

Imy Verjee

Around the dying rose,
Lie bleeding Trojan woes.
When Sinon did deceive,
He glory would receive.
For words false as the sign,
He sent when she did shine.
Who built the hateful cross,
And damned the Albatross.
Atropos cuts the thread,
And I am left for dead.
Three faces turn on me,
That branded Cain did see.
"Embrace the second death,
The lake of fire's breath."

Confessions to Cierra

A roof that caves beneath the hand of fate
Is ill prepared to bear the pouring rain;
Love clings to broken dreams within the hate,
Determined now to weather hellish pain.
No fire ever stayed the freezing tide,
Which washes Love upon uncharted shores;
He arms himself with ice to be his guide,
Determined now to fight the Spinners' wars.
With every heart that beats to touch the sky,
He stands still firm upon the falling ground;
One enemy is Fear, who stays the cry,
And turns the prey into the savage hound.
Now roads diverge and Love can win or lose,
Step clear away or burn to light the fuse.

Imy Verjee

Love treads infertile ground to nurse his seed,
Once planted in the heart he begs it grow;
Awoken by the sun which set so low,
He has resolved to right my foolish deed.
Within my breast his sacred soldiers breed,
To waking dreams they do her vision show;
Her touch allows immortal blood to flow,
She fulfils each desire, every need.
A faithful servant with his master dies,
Like some brave captain on a cursed ship,
To Love I pledge to give my life entire.
O'er seas full treacherous are blessed skies,
Yet each horizon is a poisoned lip,
Her kiss does lie across the funeral pyre.

Confessions to Cierra

No creature born of dust can just presume
To gods defy, nor mallet wield as judge;
The raven will with birth still life consume,
A fallen seed for blood can bear no grudge.
I have been born and dead at Heaven's will,
And fuel for anger is the devil's grace;
She came with Him, my blood for her did spill,
His loving heart I saw within her face.
There is a plan immortal in His mind,
To this brief wisdom must I ever cling,
Full faith alone does peaceful sleep allow.
She is the fire built for me to find,
The love of Heaven would my Cierra bring,
For her I do repent, renew my vow.

Dear Jack,

Every night bro, every night I lie down and I think, I think how can this be my God how can it be this way? To be as accurate as I can possibly be in this the most trying time that you and me we've ever sat down over three thousand miles to discuss I must tell you that I have this day received the most incredible revelation that I have had in my life - and it is not the most incredible revelation that I thought I had had, you see I lost my way I did, it was lost and I didn't know it was lost I thought it was found but I was wrong so wrong. I thought, I thought that I had been forsaken I thought that I had been cast aside I thought the birds had screamed. Had flown right by I thought the black-winged gulls, I thought I saw them fly and I was lost and lost and torn and torn and shoved aside and left and there I was and I was born and I was new and I had serpent blood and His was a serpent's heart and things were never what they seem to be, you see I thought I knew I thought that it was life and it was truth, true naked truth revealed and I had seen the light and seen the truth revealed and so I left the ship deserted it and living death came down and kissed my mouth and that was once my revelation.

But now, now my friend I see the lies the truth for all the lies. I see the world - in beauty passed that which would possess that took my heart and sunk the depths of chaos, man the frozen ice of hell is not the life the air the rain the snow the flower and the shade. It isn't so, but now I know that I don't know I don't know who or why or if I am and in confusion (which they say if they can be believed or if they even believe in what they say they say confusion is the demon's seed) I have no thought of clarity no place of strength and light no crystal vision. And night after night I know that I can bleed but I don't want the blood and I don't want to bleed and do not want to draw the blood. They, them, that great conspiracy of gods that I accused accursed and did forever damn. But not forever, no not damnation. I don't have the path nor know what I should do but this - I can no longer grieve for this, this truth this life this love this every word.

Now brother I don't know what to do. I'm back, I'm hers I'm here I'm back again. I'm mystic drawn, she the artist, and my God alive she Jack she beats my heart but if only. Man there is no way there is no way that this is something to dismiss that she went by my mind - my God she went right through my heart. It can't be true I have to love her, there's nothing left of me and now it's been three years three years gone by and in those years I've seen the light of hope and in her eyes the Heaven's place and love just love that beats the words and blows your mind and knocks you down and picks you up and beats you in the wind and winds that ever blow and blow and blow and make you scream and lose your head to find your heart and find that midnight parade that makes you run and laugh and feel.

It's not too late, it can't be, cannot be I don't know what to do, but it can't be, I, no, I, it will not cannot, it can't happen, will not no, will not be, that way is not the way. I can't have been so accursed for one mistake that one mistake. I spent last night falling in love again and she came down again and we held hands again and I looked into her eyes again, the same moon rose last night and every night and every night I fall in love again. But I can't hold her hand and I can't hold her tight and I can't speak the words that I was born to speak, what can I do bro, what can I do? The revelation that I had, man I woke up and saw that I was left to fall but as I fell I paid the other side of love - Cierra came and I saw the rising sun and as I fell I saw it set and God, what can He think what can He think of me who fell so far so far I pray but He what can He think about that box that box that cursed box that opened up and very nearly caught and trapped and I don't know. I don't know.

But in this moment in this candle's glow I see what wasn't in that liquid needle or that broken bottle, it wasn't in that burning plant but man that seemed the way to go you know not right but just the way and now I see. I can't leave, I can't go, I can't say goodbye, because I wasn't meant to leave I wasn't meant to go I wasn't meant to say goodbye and if there was ever a violation of holy law or ever a violation of holy word of spiritual life, but all I know, all I know is this. I love her Jack, I love her, I, I do, that's all.

Confessions to Cierra

When first my eyes did light upon your hair,
Which fell so free as Eden's river flows,
I knew the Fates had cut their thread with care,
Had written me a part that Troilus knows.
And then to see you turn, and catch your eye,
It seemed that Love had spent his every dart;
To be assured that this would never die
He emptied every quill into my heart.
When with regret the earth did move again,
Still I could feel your hand in soft caress,
There was a sigh from every wooded glen,
Where Muses lie awake, they lovers bless.
Forever branded on my woken mind
Is your true love, which Heaven let me find.

Imy Verjee

You dominate my life, it is for you
That I do draw the air and sweet embrace
Each pleasant cloud, which laughing lovers chase.
When falling leaves descend with winter true
And empty are the trees of summer dew,
The only sun that rises warms their place;
With thoughts of you the branches fill, solace
Is found in barren cold from Heaven's view.
You play upon the sky and sea, like heat
Provided earth by some insurgent god,
Who loving would the wrath of Heaven bear.
Fit for immortal life are you, whose seat
Is placed at Jove's right hand, the gods applaud
Their finest work, no mortal made so fair.

Confessions to Cierra

Such loving warmth is found within your heart,
For all the beauty that does lie without;
Your shining skin sees angels dance about,
Yet beauty lies within the greater part.
It is your spirit pure that caps his dart,
Brings forth sweet falling rain to heal the drought;
Now every mountain plays the echoed shout
Of this completed soul once torn apart.
Born naked to the earth, I am complete,
With wisdom of our true eternal bond,
We have forever been, and yet will be.
Two spirits did descend, on earth to meet,
True magic is not in the waving wand,
But rather rests in love you woke in me.

Imy Verjee

The world I know I would surrender now,
All things possessed, and closest to my heart,
If only our true love he would allow,
Red Love would honour his anointed dart.
You fall into my life with every sleep,
And when I lie awake you hold my mind;
The bending willow branch would joyful weep,
If warmth like yours it could in sunlight find.
That wraith who lies along the demon rim,
Who did the strength of Jupiter deny,
Would his proud blasphemy recant to him
For but one chance to catch your gleaming eye.
No demon of Judecca born to hate
Could break these words, they have been sown by fate.

Confessions to Cierra

Come sit beside me, as you came before,
In dreams I see you standing at the door.
The world did stop, if only for five days,
Since then I've walked while every poet prays.
They beg the Muses for a tale to tell
Of my redemption from this living hell.
For every day that fades to disappear
They shed another and still truer tear.
No love like ours can be by mortals sent,
It must be true, and have a god's consent.
For Helen did the Trojan War take place,
Each ship would sail again to win your grace.
Yet every sky is but another wall,
No sun is seen to either rise or fall.

Imy Verjee

Red satin shield
Descends into this field;
To arm my heart,
Reclaim the missing part.
The arrow's head
Was forged from golden thread;
It did true land,
As from Apollo's hand.
You are the light,
No morning star so bright;
It has to be
That Venus hears this plea.
Eternal chains,
Bound God Himself complains.

Confessions to Cierra

The nightingale awakes,
She sweetest grief;
Each sunlit tree He shakes
To shed a leaf.
Slow falling in the wind,
Caught by your breath;
It blows for those who sinned,
Preventing death.
Two hands extended cry,
The blood of woe;
A second sun is high,
The first to show.
False prophets born to lie,
Run off and die.

Imy Verjee

The shelter of your wings fierce fans the flame,
No sun above provides such burning heat;
In you I have found knowledge of His name,
Which drives life-bearing wind with love complete.
The angels' clothing do you graceful wear,
Both skin and spirit cast of holy clay;
Each star competes to shine within your hair,
And with your waking Dawn revives the day.
That you were made did cause me be unmade,
'Till resurrection breathes in settled sand;
A desert Phoenix living as a shade,
Awaiting life which lies at your command.
When Heaven does fulfil its holy plan,
Two severed lives will join one soul again.

Confessions to Cierra

I love you now, as much as then,
I've tried to tell you live and now with pen.
The game is done, this player bust,
What's left of me is ashes, living dust.
But memories we've made and kept,
With you in mind each night I've peaceful slept.
And now, no miracle in sight,
The time has come to fall, perhaps take flight.
My love upon your sacred heart,
Beware the god, and mind his poisoned dart.
Please know I always meant to try,
But every trick of fate did words deny.
In Heaven, if the tale is true,
We'll have our dance, and always I'll love you.

Imy Verjee

Dear Jack,

One more time, man, one more time the merry-go-round goes 'round and 'round. And every time it goes full circle every time that ring goes 'round the pack it thins out just a little bit more man a little bit more. This whole wild pack of horses runnin' free and just roamin' and groovin' and blowin' across the land and the oceans, and the sky across the sky and one by one they just fall off you know one by one they just fall off and one by one they just get dropped by some wild hunter out there just cuttin' them down and cuttin' you down and the pack it loses one every time around and time after time he's thinnin' them down and thinnin' them down and they have to slow down 'till there's just one. The pack's all gone 'cause there's just one. The light the lovely light angelic light the demon light it takes and takes and wild crazy madness of the pack it's lost a step to see the light and ever-slower ever-slower 'till one last step and then another horse falls and another last step and a thinned-out pack and one by one they fall and one by one they slow and then there's just one left one crazy horse who can't be crazy anymore can't explode anymore so he just stands still he just looks out at the sea 'cause he can't run anymore and he can't swim anymore. Just starin' at the sky.

And that sky, it's like it adds a cloud for every fallen horse and ever fallen seraph light. The wide blue sky it learns the cloud and then the cloud it forms a film and then the mist and mist that takes the fallen horses breeding fog a falling fog that covers the mist and covers the sky and falls and sinks and keeps falling onto that one horse that's left on the beach can't you see him all covered in fog and covered and nothing to touch and nothing to hold and nothing to see he can't see. And as that merry-go-round it spins and slows that ring its gone the horse it stops it has to stop. At first you know you think you know for all the fog the ring's still there and one more horse and more cloud and then one morning it could be there it could still be but one more day and maybe you think it's gone one more day and

97

maybe it's gone and one more day for that and it's gone it's gone and nothing not even mist for fog and night the darkness night and nothing to see and the water so unclear. And so you fall.

Imy Verjee

I do submit before the weaving Fates,
Immersed within the waves of river Hate.
The Baptist never knew such liquid force
As did through brave Achilleus living course;
It burns the candle bright with breathing flame,
He died immortal, fortunate in fame,
Who took his place as king amongst the dead,
Would never serve the god for whom he bled.
So do I now emerge with skin repaired,
Red Love can die again for all who cared;
Those lovers who were never meant to kiss,
But forced apart anticipating bliss.
With Chaos and with Night the demons rise,
To take the Kingdom from the Tyrant's lies.

Confessions to Cierra

A bottle falling,
An angel calling.
Empty halls that cry,
Broken walls deny.
Pray to Love tonight,
Stay within the light.
In fright is the Muse,
The fight will refuse.
God unmoved to care,
Will not freedom share,
The daring demon,
Serpent seraphim.
Broken yellow leaves,
Every poet grieves.

Imy Verjee

Last call arrives, does at my table sit,
No end in sight, now every door is shut;
Without a second dart my heart is cut,
To fight a war for her I am not fit.
Dawn trembles scared, and will to Night submit,
Who drives me like a snake into this rut;
Desire fails, provides nor fruit nor nut
To starving Lovers broken by the bit.
Inside a jug of punch I helpless drown,
Once sacred things are lost, forever turned
Against this helpless child whom Love betrayed.
Both far and wide her beauty is renowned,
For her I built this pyre, willing burned
To wander lifeless, as at last I strayed.

Confessions to Cierra

He said a snail did crawl along the edge,
To brave a razor built to draw its blood;
They say he is insane to make his pledge,
Forsake the arc to join the lethal flood.
He said he saw the beauty in the beast,
The strength to take the arm equipped to heal;
They say he has been damaged by the feast,
Embracing wisdom with his final meal.
He said an errand boy was sent by clerks,
To claim an unpaid debt which stained the book;
They say he every Godly moral shirks,
Will wander aimless for the path he took.
Insanity is but a preacher's card,
Played by the sheep who find the truth too hard.

Imy Verjee

A victim poised to strike the cursed air
Is not protected by Amazing Grace;
Each river dries, all trees of fruit are bare,
Unearthly sand does mask her holy face.
Time unchecked maintains a dreary beat,
With little thought to those beneath the tread;
Now vengeful is the field stripped bare of wheat,
It rises from the grave, the lover's bed.
Upon the shoulders of the god called Love
I press the weight of his unfeeling dart;
Although no grant afforded from above,
I will with justice due me burn his heart.
To war with gods is said risk the life,
But living death, this night I hold the knife.

Confessions to Cierra

Silver shining,
The sunlit tempered blade;
Angels crying,
This path He fierce forbade.
A length of rope
Is freedom from the cold;
In blindness grope
For promises He sold.
Breaking bottle,
The peaceful pills within;
Vengeance throttle,
He cannot bear the sin.
The saddened heart,
Yet He did write this part.

Imy Verjee

A weapon cocked is waiting for the sign,
Its single silver shell entreats release;
Another fading moon without a sign,
Dark Heaven's brow does in a prayer crease.
But this revolving door the light provides,
While Aphrodite's son remains unseen;
When sought he disappears amongst the tides,
Upon the barrel does my forehead lean.
Slow tracing down for yet a better fit,
Across my brow and slowly past the cheek;
It damp decides beneath my chin to sit,
Through death the lovers' life immortal seek.
One final glance to catch the eye above,
If He would just make good his words of love.

Confessions to Cierra

A needle fills with Love, in liquid red,
Which drawn and poised prepares a life to take;
God watches with a smile, as on a bed
The poisoned droplets flow into the lake.
The deed once done unites pain Heavenly
With pleasure's tears within a stricken mind;
To breathe but take no air is misery
Which pales before a weary lover's bind.
'Tis said that tunnels are by Heaven lit,
When Death is given his due audience;
But every Fate that has my prison knit,
Allows no guilt removed by penitence.
"I preach'd, as never sure to preach again;
And as a dying Man to dying Men."

Dear Stacey,

One last night, my friend. Finally left alone, a room with every socket bare, cords and plugs are scattered on the floor. As I write this note, the end, this note, I'm just waiting for a final look at that old sun, that old friend of mine. It seems so dull these days, I just want to see it shine again. It all seems so dull, though, I don't know, even the candles don't want to burn tonight. I guess they don't much care anymore. It's funny, you know, I remember the first car we had, my folks had, when I was just a kid. Must've been only a couple of years old when we got it, this old '79 Honda Civic. Had a hatchback looked like some wild spaceship to a kid, looked like the safest little thing in the world, gold paintjob and man, every year, every winter, every northern snow that fell it'd keep right on goin'. Such a little thing, that bug of a car, and so easily dismissed, but man it had a living heart and just kept on and I don't know. Just this little beat-up old Civic with so many clicks on it you know it must've been around a thousand years, a little tiny gold-shelled thing scratched up by rust and rain and still it moved and you knew you were safe and you knew it kept you safe.

It's funny what you remember, but sometimes my mom, she used to talk about driving home with us kids in the back, my brother and me, in the middle of a snowstorm. And she'd tell us stories about gettin' caught out there, the little car stalled out, and everybody in a panic, and our gettin all covered, windows n' all, in blowing snow, so bad we couldn't see and her trying and the engine coughing. But I don't remember that, not once, for me that car always made good, always kept going and always stayed warm, snow and all. Until the last day, the day we gave it up, I'd grown up with it, and it with me, and I guess it knew what we were doing, I guess it knew that we were leaving, 'cause that day we took in, it stalled and stalled, and just stopped and died so that it didn't have to die. It wanted so bad to live, you know, it just wanted to be where it had been, and man it tried.

Confessions to Cierra

I hope that you can understand this. I tried too, I did, with every breath of life. Hell. I guess I gave her my life a long time ago, four years ago. You know, they say Dido killed herself for love, stabbed herself right there on her funeral pyre. They say she built it herself, laid right down on it, and died for love. I only wish this could be that way, could have some seed of that romance, some of that mystic air. But, this night, these fading candles, this starless sky... it just doesn't have the feeling they say she felt. So, why; why? You ask me, I ask God, I guess the answer's pretty much the same. Not much of anything. I guess I got my kicks and dug my life as best I could. You know, when that bright-blue centre-light dies out, there just isn't anything left to do but fall out of the sky.

Imy Verjee

All that I was in love was fate's design,
Those three immortal gods did hold the reins;
With many spoken words and sad refrains
The poet prayed, yet water is not wine.
Though mortals never know of plans divine
I still did beg the gods to lift their banes;
All sacrifice to Love, whose dart ordains,
The lover cried, yet shadows do not shine.
Now Dawn of braided hair the new day brings,
She does renew those hearts Love has not torn,
And paints their skies with soft rose-coloured light.
The rest are left behind, no angel sings,
But thank you Cierra, for I was twice born;
I bless you God, and kiss eternal night.

Confessions to Cierra

About the Author

Imy Verjee was born in Nairobi, Kenya, in 1975, the younger of two children. Moving with his family as a boy, he would settle after several years in Toronto, Canada. He attended local schools, and a local university; during these later years, he would begin a succession of restless travels, initially driven by a desire for flight rather than an attraction to any particular destination. It was on one of these journeys that he would first discover the only place to which he has since returned for an extended length of time, Northern Ireland. It was here that he began *Confessions to Cierra*, his first work.

With the shadow of Petrarch rising to fall over his writings, each word of every line is produced with a particular reader in mind, his confessor. Imy has long been a reverent admirer of the revolutionary poets who came to define the Beat generation. Trailing along in the footsteps of those same self-proclaimed prophets, he has continued to wander across lands both foreign and domestic in physical pursuit of metaphysical self-realisation.